Titles in the series

The Air-stewardess   0–241–11209–5
The Ambulancewoman   0–241–11680–5
The Car Mechanic   0–241–11663–5
The Chef   0–241–11661–9
The Dustman   0–241–11210–9
The Doctor   0–241–11415–2
The Farmer   0–241–10937–X
The Fireman   0–241–10936–1
The Fisherman   0–241–11414–4
The Hairdresser   2–241–11211–7
The Helicopter Pilot   0–241–11662–7
The Lorry-driver   0–241–11164–1
The Milkman   0–241–10934–5
The Nurse   0–241–11162–5
The Policewoman   0–241–10935–3
The Postman   0–241–11163–3
The Shop-keeper   0–241–11416–0
The Soldier   0–241–11417–9
The Vet   0–241–11165–X
The Zoo-keeper   0–241–11212–5

The author and publishers would like to thank Hugh Watkis, the management and staff at Henlys (West) Ltd, Bristol, and the Austin Rover Group for their assistance with this book.

Layout by Andrew Shoolbred

First published in Great Britain 1985 by
Hamish Hamilton Children's Books
Garden House, 57–59 Long Acre, London WC2E 9JZ
Copyright © 1985 by Hamish Hamilton Ltd.
All rights reserved

British Library Cataloguing in Publication Data
Stewart, Anne
The Car Mechanic.—(Cherrystones)

Typeset by Katerprint Co. Ltd, Oxford

Printed in Great Britain by
Cambus Litho, East Kilbride

The Car Mechanic

Anne Stewart

Photographs by
Chris Fairclough

Hamish Hamilton · London

It is 8.30 on a cold, dark morning in December and Hugh Watkis is clocking on for work. Hugh works as a mechanic in a big Austin Rover garage in Bristol. Most of the cars the mechanics work on are made by Austin Rover. You can see the company's badge on Hugh's overall.

Hugh reports to Ken the foreman to find out his jobs for the day. Ken gives him a card, called a ticket, for each job The ticket lists exactly what needs to be done. The work may involve repairing or replacing a faulty part, or servicing a car to make sure everything is in good running order.

Hugh walks to his work bench and unlocks his tool box. A complete set of tools is very expensive and each mechanic has to buy his own. A few months ago, thieves broke into the garage and stole Hugh's tool box. It was never found and Hugh had to buy a new set of tools. Now his tool box is bolted to the work bench.

Today's first job is to service an Austin Metro. This means checking the electrical and mechanical parts of the car. It also means replacing some of the parts, even if they appear to be in good condition.

All Metros should be serviced at least once a year, or every 19,000 kilometres – whichever comes first.

Hugh begins by checking the rubber blades on the windscreen wipers. If they are worn, they will not clean the windscreen properly.

Then he checks the headlamps. He measures the height and direction of the beams to make sure they are not too high. Otherwise, they may dazzle drivers coming from the opposite direction. Both beams should point slightly towards the nearside kerb.

It is important that the wheels are 'tracking' properly. If they are not positioned at exactly the right angle, the driver may find it hard to steer properly. It is difficult to check the wheels by eye, so Hugh uses a special measure called a tracking gauge.

It is easier to check some parts of a car when it is on a ramp. This is a steel platform which can be raised or lowered to suit the mechanic. Hugh carefully drives the car into position. He has covered the car seat with plastic so that it won't get dirty.

Hugh pushes a lever and the ramp automatically goes up. As soon as he lets go, the ramp stops still.

Hugh makes sure the tyres are in good condition, and then removes each wheel in turn. He uses a special 'gun' called a torque wrench to loosen the nuts.

Now the brakes must be checked. Cars have two different kinds of brakes, one for the front and one for the back. Those at the front are called disc brakes. This is because a thick round plate (or disc) of steel is attached to the wheel. When the driver presses on the brake pedal, brake pads on either side of the disc press inwards and slow down the wheel. The brake pads are inside the box Hugh holds in his right hand.

The brakes at the back are called drum brakes. This time, when the brake pedal is pressed, two brake 'shoes' press against the inside of the drum. The drum slows down, and so does the wheel. The shoes are covered with a tough lining which slowly wears away. Hugh takes off the drum case to see if the lining needs replacing.

Whenever a car is given a major service, it must have an oil change. No car's engine will run smoothly unless all its moving parts are coated in dirt-free oil. Hugh raises the ramp to its fullest height, and stands directly beneath the car. He unscrews a cap and the oil pours into a large funnel, and on into a big metal barrel.

When all the oil has drained out, Hugh goes to the store room to collect two tins of fresh oil and some spare parts. As Andy fetches the different items, Bob notes them down in his record book. When the list is complete, Hugh signs it at the bottom.

Hugh lowers the ramp to the ground and pours in the fresh oil. This car takes about 4½ litres. To avoid splashing the engine with oil, Hugh pours it through a funnel.

Spark plugs must also be changed during a major service. The Metro has four, while other cars have six, eight or twelve. The plugs are fitted near the front of the engine where they can be easily reached. Although they are quite small, they are very important. Without them, the engine would be unable to make any power to drive the car.

Most cars are fuelled by petrol. The petrol is pumped to the carburettor, where it mixes with air to form a kind of explosive gas. The gas is lit by a spark from a spark plug so that it expands and forces other parts of the engine to move. The power from the engine is then taken to the driving wheels – and the car can move.

In order for the engine to run smoothly, it must be kept clean. So an air filter is fitted to the carburettor to catch any specks of dirt. Look how dirty this used filter is!

When Hugh finishes the service, he signs the ticket and takes the car for a test drive. If everything runs smoothly, he parks the car in the garage forecourt. The foreman then checks it and telephones the customer to say the car is ready.

At about midday, Hugh takes a half-hour break for lunch. He can choose when to have a rest, so he usually waits until he has finished a job. But first he must wash his hands. They are covered in oil and grease. He uses a special jelly-like soap.

'When I first started work in a garage,' Hugh says, 'no one told me there was a special soap you could use. I spent ages scrubbing my hands and still couldn't get them clean. I nearly didn't become a mechanic because of that!'

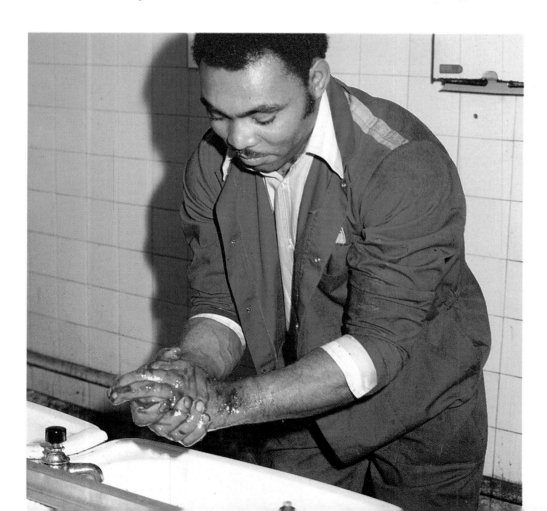

Hugh and the other mechanics buy their lunch from Joyce. She comes to the garage every day to make sandwiches, rolls and hot dogs. She also sells cups of tea and coffee, cake, crisps and chocolate.

'Bit on the cold side today,' says Joyce. 'I expect you're looking forward to your holiday.' Hugh is taking his family to Jamaica in February. It is only the second time he has been back since he left at the age of ten. His daughters have never been there.

'Yes, it should be nice and warm,' Hugh agrees. 'And it will be lovely to see my relatives again.'

The mechanics usually work on their own. But sometimes they need help. Lifting an engine in and out of a car is always a difficult job. Engines are very heavy and awkward to move.

Hugh and Derek have lifted this engine out of a Maxi so that Hugh can work on the gear box. In this kind of car, the engine fits on top of the gear box. This is called a transverse engine. In some other cars, the gear box fits behind the engine.

Hugh begins to examine the gear box. Inside, there are a number of gear wheels, or gears. Most cars have four or five forward gears and one reverse gear. They link the engine with the driving wheels.

Depending on which gear is used, the car travels within a particular range of speeds. The lowest gear, the first, is used for speeds up to 5 m.p.h. The top gear, the fourth (or sometimes, the fifth), is used for speeds of 30 m.p.h. and over. When a driver wants to change from one gear to the next, he or she simply presses the foot pedal called the clutch and moves the gear stick to the gear required.

The mechanics have to be prepared to work in uncomfortable positions. Some parts of a car cannot be reached in any other way. Hugh and Derek have just removed the rear axle from a Rover. (The rear axle connects the two back wheels, and links them to the engine.) Hugh has decided not to use the ramp because he will have to work under the car for a long time. Under a ramp, he would quickly get neckache.

'Why do you always get the easy job, Derek?' Hugh jokes.

Hugh discovers the brake pipes are worn and decides to replace them. When the brake pedal is pressed down, brake fluid is forced along pipes to each of the four wheels. The fluid presses against the small metal cylinder (called a piston) and this forces the brake pads or shoes to slow down the wheels. For safety reasons, it is very important that the brake pipes are in good condition.

Although Hugh is a mechanic, he enjoys trim work too. This involves repairing interior parts, and fitting extras inside the car – for example, seat belts and baby seats. The door pad on this Mini is loose. Hugh spreads a piece of clean paper on the work bench and lays the pad on it, innerside up. Then he dots special glue all over it.

When the glue feels sticky, Hugh slips the pad back into place. He makes sure there are no drips.

At half past five, Hugh tidies his tool box and locks it. He
washes his hands and takes off his overalls. He hangs
them in his locker. Every Monday he puts on a clean pair.
He calls goodbye to Derek and the other mechanics and
walks the few minutes back home.

Hugh spends a lot of his free time at church. He belongs to the Pentecostal Church and every Friday evening the congregation meets in a school hall. Hugh plays the accordion while everyone else sings and claps hands. Sometimes people raise their hands and shout 'Hallelujah!'. It is a joyful service and for Hugh the most important time of the week.

Index

air filter	13
brakes	8–9, 21
gear box	16–19
headlamps	5
oil change	10–11
servicing (a car)	4–13
spark plugs	12
trim work	8
windscreen wipers	4